STORAGE AUCTION RESALE GUIDE

MIKE & AMY MAROHL

Published by:

Daylight Publishing

Rockland, WI USA

608-451-0059

DEDICATION

This book is dedicated to our eight children: Marissa, Mattingly, Mercedes, Maris, Miranda, Mason, Mitchell and Megan. You are all our wonderful helpers and we enjoy your entrepreneurial "can do" attitudes. Without you all, this business would not be possible. We love each of you dearly.

CONTENTS

INTRODUCTION

We, the authors, took a gamble in 2013 and started buying abandoned storage units and selling the items within to make money and now you can too! This book will help educate you on how this business works so you can try it and have a much faster learning curve than we did.

You will learn how to consider the costs of startup, find the auctions, auction etiquette, what happens at an auction, how to store the items, how to wisely go through the items and sort them, what to do with photographs, how to sell each type of item, what to do with items that won't sell and how to keep track of business income and expenses for tax purposes.

Our family had to learn this the hard way and we felt like there should be a book about this to make it easier for newcomers. We felt a burden to write this book, so you won't have to feel that way. Also, when people ask what we do for a living, they are not at all curious about Mike's full-time day job, but everyone wants to know about the part time storage unit business! The conversation can sometimes turn into an hour, so we thought it would be nice to have a book to offer them. Keep in mind that our auctions are in Wisconsin and Minnesota because they are all within a few hours of where we live. Your auction experience may be different than ours and we hope you will write about it too.

This business works for our family because currently (2019), Mike works a full-time day job at a cable television business and Amy is an author, homeschooling homemaker, blogger at neededinthehome.com and Etsy shop owner of NeededInTheHome. We presently have eight children and the older ones help us with the storage unit business or babysitting while we are busy with auctions or moving items and they are paid for it.

There is a popular television show called, *Storage Wars*. On that show, the buyers lose money or gain money depending on what they find in their units. We want to show you that every unit has the potential to earn money if you are willing to work for it. **Many** items in a unit have the potential for resale. Not just a **few** items as featured on *Storage Wars*. It just depends on how willing you are to do the work to "move" the stuff. Now it's time to learn, let's start making money with these storage auction resale secrets!

CHAPTER ONE
PREPARING TO BUY

Do you like treasure hunting? How about "grab bags" with a mystery prize inside? Wouldn't it be great to get a 10 foot by 10-foot grab bag? This is the fun part of this business. You never know what you will find. It might be something you have been searching for at a rummage sale and auctions for years.

Let's ask some personal questions here. Do you get queasy looking at other people's dirty clothing, or their garbage? Does the smell of stale cigarette smoke, human sweat, cheap cologne/perfume, or rotten food make you sick? If that is the case, you will have to learn to get tough and make yourself like steel so you can get through this.

Sadly, not everyone stores their items in a clean and organized way. Even when a unit looks like it has been moved by a moving company and looks very organized, labeled, etc., you will still find these things. Moving companies have it in their policy to move everything. They will pack the garbage and the contents of the refrigerator, so when you open the Tupperware you know you can resell on eBay or Amazon, you may find rotten food. (We'll get into eyeing cleaner, better quality units later.)

It does comfort us to know that we should not find lice or fleas, and we haven't. Usually, at least in our area, the storage unit company has given their client *plenty* of time to pay, months or years, before they put the unit up for auction. That is too long for lice or fleas to survive.

However, the owners of storage unit companies are human. Sadly, humans have been known to make mistakes. A friend of ours who also purchases units told us of a time that he purchased a unit and started selling off the contents when he received a phone call from the storage unit company that the sale had been a mistake, they sold the wrong person's stuff. So, in that extremely rare case, you might find lice or fleas!

In that situation, the unit purchaser was paid back the amount he paid for the unit and he was able to keep the funds from the items he already did sell. He chose to give the owners the rest of the items, which he had already done the work to move to his town. Every business has problems. Thankfully, we have never had that happen.

Realize that you may find items that are mature in nature. Have a plan for swiftly dealing with these items, especially if you have children with you. We purchase latex gloves to wear when going through units because you just never know what you will find.

Can you handle it emotionally? You will accidentally find out about the previous owner's lifestyle: their problems and successful experiences. You may find out that a man died due to health and he was alone and had no family to claim his stuff.

Let's say you feel like you could handle the above-mentioned items. That's great because the other side of this can be very promising. The positive out of these "bad situations" is that the people who cannot claim their units may leave very valuable items behind. Some items have been in their family for years, some are piggy banks, old purses, jewelry or fire safe locked boxes with cash you can take right to the bank!

CHAPTER TWO
TIME AND SPACE ISSUES

Let's talk about time. Some auctions are on a Tuesday morning. If you work a Monday through Friday daytime job and have children's sporting and church events all week in the evenings, do you really have time to get out of the unit before the deadline? Some Unit businesses want the auction purchaser completely out of the unit by noon the next day.

Every storage unit business owner is different. Some will give you more time if you ask. Ask the owner, sometimes the auctioneer is not the owner and cannot give permission for that. They may give it to you through the weekend just for asking. That is not uncommon.

Sometimes, if you want more time, you must pay to rent it. Some will let you rent by the week. Others are by the month, even if you are out of it early. Because of our busy lives, there have been times that we could not attend auctions because of lack of time to go through them.

We prefer a Tuesday morning auction because there is less competition and we get a lower price. On a Saturday auction, we see ten times the amount of competition and we end up paying more for the unit that we want.

4

Do you have a place to bring the items to until you can sell them or sort through them? How large is your storage space? That answer may tell you what size of a unit to purchase or how many you can purchase.

If you have a small garden shed that would hold a riding lawn mower, you will not want to bid on a large 10 foot by 20-foot unit packed full of items unless you plan on renting that unit for a while. We will talk more about storage later.

What if the unit you purchase has furniture items in it? If they don't sell right away, you will need a place to keep them out of the weather. If you have little storage space, you may have a disadvantage in this business. You will have to incur more costs with renting the unit; or, wait for a smaller unit to bid on.

You may not see a smaller unit until next month, or a few months. This problem could be solved by taking large items right to the dump, which in our area costs extra money, plus you miss out on making money back on the resell-able large items.

CHAPTER THREE
MONEY AND BUDGETING

When we started, we didn't have any extra money, things were tight. We waited for our tax return money to arrive. When it did, we set aside a small amount from that check for the storage unit business.

How much money will you need? You will need money for the auction itself. We have purchased units as low as one dollar and have seen them go for thousands. It could be higher in other states and depends on your competition's budget.

Decide on what you can afford to lose. In our area, we are not allowed to go inside the unit or to open anything until we have purchased it. Many items are in boxes, bags, or suitcases. We bid with an assumption that we will make a certain amount of dollars back on a unit.

We count the boxes/bags/suitcases and estimate an approximate resale value. This is a gamble. We may not make the money back. It is possible that every box or bag in the unit contains worthless items.

Sometimes, all you can see is cardboard boxes and you open them to find clothing in all of them with stains, rips and holes and you cannot resell them.

Every once in a while, you will find one box that has a valuable item inside that you can resell and make your money back on the entire unit from just that box.

Consider a limit that is comfortable for you to lose *if* you get a bad one. Out of the many storage units we have purchased, we have only gotten "burned" a few times so a bad one is unlikely to happen. Normally the ones that are bad are not bought by anybody.

From the television show, Storage Wars, they most likely show you **the best** out of very *many* units up for auction that day. Very rarely do you see the bad ones because people that buy units on a regular basis don't buy the bad ones.

Now consider additional expenses for auction day. You will need a way to haul the items you win. Many storage unit businesses only give you until noon the next day to empty the locker. Do you drive there with a trailer or truck to start hauling items, even though you may not win an auction that day? If it is far away, it would be wise to do this. If it is nearby, you could win the auction, take as much stuff you can fit in the vehicle you came in and then come back to get your stuff with the trailer or truck. What if you don't have a trailer or truck? Can you borrow one? If not, you will need to research how much it would cost to rent one. Will you need to pay for extra time and rent this unit?

Sometimes the auctions are a *caravan auction*, which means that a large storage unit company that owns units in different locations will have them all on the same day. You start at one location in one town, then drive to the next location. Sometimes they are in the same area, just a few miles from each other. Sometimes they are 45 minutes apart in another town or city.

You need to follow the caravan, or you won't get to bid. During these, you don't have time to stop for the bathroom or a bite to eat or you will miss a location and if they leave too soon and you don't have a list of where they are going to next, then you will be done bidding for the day.

You will also need to plan to bring beverages and snacks. It is possible that you may need to eat out if your last auction is an hour or two away from home and it is dinner time.

Don't forget your buddy! It is very difficult to do this business alone. You need someone to help you lift the big items and it is safer to travel in a pair. Make sure you keep your help fed and hydrated. Plan for those food/drink costs.

When you plan the gas money portion of the budget, plan for several trips if necessary. Consider if you will be hauling a trailer or using a rented or borrowed truck and how much extra gas it might take. Will your buddy be bringing his/her own vehicle and/or trailer for your benefit? You may want to put gas in that vehicle too. It is kind of like when you are moving from one house or apartment to another.

Purchase some quality locks to put on the unit when you win. The stuff is yours now, you need to keep it locked up until you get it out. What kind should you purchase? That is for you to decide. We recommend that you go to a storage unit facility in your area and take a look at the locks people are already using and see what you feel would be best. Some storage unit businesses will make you use their locks and you have to go to their office to ask for the key and return it when you are done. But it is most likely that you will have to use your own so come prepared.

There are some other items you should bring with you. Bring rubber gloves and garbage bags. Believe it or not, some people are not as organized as you and just throw their stuff into the unit, maybe in a hurry. It is not boxed and you may find broken bottles of cologne or oil. Sometimes, you have to go inside a building and the hallway is not well-lit and the unit inside has no lighting; so be sure you bring a quality flashlight or other light.

In making out your budget, you will take a guess at how much all the items listed above add up to be. In the Auction Budget provided, pencil in these numbers. Keep the total at an amount you can afford to take a risk of loss on.

Auction Budget

Items	Amount
Storage Unit(s) You Win	
Renting the Unit(s) for more time	
Truck/Trailer rental	
Gas	
Garbage/Recycling Fees	
Buddy/Helper (pay, meals, gas)	
Meals	
Misc. (locks, gloves, garbage bags, light, tape measure)	
Other	
Total =	

Now your bid limit is the amount in the "Storage Unit(s) You Win" section. Do not bid higher than that unit amount and remember to adjust it mentally if you see a lot of garbage, mattresses, or TV sets that you may have to dispose of. Also adjust if you think hauling or gas will be more money.

Bring your total amount in cash and get receipts for everything, even if you have to drive to their main office to get the receipt. There are very few auctions that we know of in our area (Wisconsin, USA) that accept any other form of payment besides cash and you usually have to develop a relationship with the owner before they would accept a check. You can call their business office ahead of time to double check the form of payment accepted.

CHAPTER FOUR
WHAT TO BRING TO THE AUCTION

Smartphone with a camera

If there is a crowd, you will only get a minute to look into the unit so others can have a turn to look too. That's just enough time to snap some photos. Then get out of the way and look at the photos, enlarge the photo to read box labels or see if that really is a gun case back there. This will help you see what is there and determine how much to bid.

If others are taking a long time to look before bidding starts, you may have time to go on eBay and see what that antique board game has sold for in the past that you see in the unit. Just keep in mind, that box might be empty so don't bid too high!

After you win the unit and start going through the items, you will snap photos of large items to sell right out of the storage locker. You could even post them on Facebook, etc. right then and there.

To call your wife to see if she wants the Coach purse you found while loading up the unit. Or, to call your husband to see if he wants the poker table or laptop, etc.

To check lists in your memos to see if someone is looking for an item you can watch for while emptying the storage garage.

If your flashlight batteries aren't working, you can download an app to make your Smartphone into a flashlight.

To record in your memo the addresses and unit numbers of the auctions you win so you can find them again. You could also record your lock number so you know which key to bring.

Cash/Check/Debit Card

Most of the auctions we have been to only accept cash.

You may want another form of payment for food, gas, garbage/recycling fees or renting a truck or trailer for hauling.

You may have to pay your buddy for help or buy lunch or gas for him/her.

"Look For" or "Waiting List" or "Want To Buy" list

You can call or text someone on your "look for" list and ask, "Were you looking for a gas dryer or electric dryer?" Try to keep that list in the memos on your Smartphone. Then, you could send a photo to customers on your waiting list and they could hopefully come get the item while you are there packing up. Less to move is always good!

Moving Buddy

This could be a friend or family member who is also bidding but agree not to bid each other up. You can always buy that box of baseball cards or Ty beanie babies from him/her after it is won. Or trade it for something he/she wants out of the unit you won.

In our case, this is usually an older child who we pay commissions to. He/she also gets first dibs on treasure that we agree to let them keep.

It's nice to have someone to help lift heavy items or hold a flashlight.

Food and Water

Always have water so you can stay hydrated, even in the winter.

In a caravan sale (you follow the group from one location to another, which can go on several hours if some locations are in other towns) you may not have time to stop for food because you could risk losing the group you are following. Or, if they gave you a list of each location in order, you might have to miss a few units being auctioned if you stop to eat.

Locks and Keys

Be sure to bring locks and keys. Don't bid on more units than you have locks for!

Sometimes, the storage facility business will make you use their lock and key and you need to return it to them, but it's best to be prepared.

Rubber Gloves

Some items are dirty or too gross for me to pick up with my bare hands.

Baby Wipes or Hand Sanitizer

You may need to wash your hands at some point.

Quality Garbage Bags

We have seen a *LOT* of garbage! Even the cleanest units that were moved with a professional moving company will have garbage.

Believe it or not, some people are not as organized as you and just throw their stuff (without a container) into the unit, maybe in a hurry. You need something to carry the keepers in and a garbage bag works. Just keep that bag separate from the bags that are going to the dump!

Flashlight

When bidding, it helps you to see in the back. Mike was at an auction that went later into the night and there were no lights to see what he was bidding on. Sometimes, you must go inside a building and the hallway is not well-lit and the unit inside has no lighting; so be sure to bring a quality flashlight or other light. The guy with the flashlight has the advantage.

When trying to empty the unit before dark, you may need it if there are a lot of items left as the sun is going down.

Tape Measure

This is helpful to see if items will fit in your vehicle or to put measurements on listings from your smartphone.

CHAPTER FIVE
FIND AND RESEARCH THE AUCTIONS

The most common question we hear when friends ask about this business is, "How do you find them?" In our state, there is a law that in order for the owner of the storage unit business to clear out the unit for the next renter, it must be published that a sale will be held. The public notice needs to be made a certain amount of days ahead of the sale and will list the location, time, date, name of the facility, name and address of the person whose goods will be auctioned off.

This gives reasonable time for the person or person's family to show up and pay the bill before the sale. It is *very* important to call the storage unit business the morning of the sale. There may be no auction that day, because everyone has come to pay the bill after being publicly embarrassed like that!

We find these notices in the local newspaper in the auctions or public notices sections. You have to read very closely, it will definitely not say, "abandoned storage unit auction". It will more likely say something like, "personal property being auctioned to settle a debt" or "a public sale will be held for the purpose of satisfying a landlord's lien. The names and last known addresses,

Storage Unit numbers and a brief description of the contents are as follows".

You can also look them up on the Internet under "public notices" for your state. Some storage unit businesses will advertise on a storage unit website. These do charge you a fee per month to be on it and we do not find very many sales this way. You can also contact the owner of each business and see if they have a mail or an email list to get on to be notified of future sales. Once you have found the auction, put it on your calendar.

Now it's time to do some research. You have a name and address on your list of people that owe money on these units along with the unit number (if your state considers this public information, like ours in Wisconsin does). Get on the internet and look up any information you can about the name and address. Sometimes you can't find anything, sometimes you can only find their age.

Recently, we learned that two different listings were for a pool and spa business. The owners have different names and addresses. Further research showed us there was more than one location to the same company and each was a branch manager. We made a mental note that if we decided to get one of these units, that we had better get the other as well. Many times, when we have only won one in a situation like this, we find half of the parts or half of the collection or half a dining room table set. It is often not in our best interest to get these because the price may go too high for the 2nd one, out of our budget range, and we have a hard time selling half a set of something. We chose not to bid on the first one after seeing it anyways, but it was good to have that information.

Often, you will see the same name and address on multiple listings up for auction and it is very obvious that they go together.

If you are going to bid, stay in your budget, but try to get them all so that you have all the pieces for resale.

In our area, one storage unit business will only sell one of their client's units at an auction in an effort to show them they are serious. This sometimes works and the person pays a lot of money to get back the remaining unit(s). If it does not work, the business auctions a second one the next month and the third, etc. in future months. If we realize we have "half a unit" (this is what we call it, though it could be a third or fourth), we look for the same owner name in future months, if we have pieces we need the other half of to sell better.

Sometimes research shows us the unit renter is in jail or has been in trouble with the law and why. Knowing this, we will be more cautious whether to bid on this unit. Often research will show us the person died and when you read the obituary, they were preceded in death by everyone and had no survivors. Sometimes these are great units and have treasures to resell. Other times, the person really has nothing but clothing, broken wheelchairs and photographs they are storing.

Rarely, you will see that the person lives in an expensive house, has a professional, high-paying job and you look forward to getting this unit, then you find out they paid it right before the auction after being publicly embarrassed. The ones you can't find any information on are usually good units with resell-able items, so don't discount them.

CHAPTER SIX
TWO AUCTIONS AT THE SAME TIME

What if you find two auctions in the same day, at about the same time? Which one should you go to? What if the auction is at the same time as another event, like taking the kids to bowling/dance/karate/club events, for example? Yes, this can happen. You may not find an auction available for three weeks, then all of a sudden you find four auctions in your travel area that are all in the same week! Worse yet, on the same day! Even worse, two are at the same time! Here is a plan for dealing with this type of situation.

After researching each sale, as mentioned in the previous section, you should have an idea of which sales you would rather go to based on what you found out. But what if there are a lot of units that you couldn't find anything on? What if there is treasure in both?

Now count **how many units are at each sale**. Keep in mind that after people have their name, address, unit number and stuff listed in the paper, they pay up quick! You may see the 12 listed in the paper go down to 4 on sale day. So if you go to the sale that has more, you should be able to have a few more to bid on. Sometimes we like to go to both, if we can, because other storage auction bidders like ourselves use this same strategy. If no one is at the sale with the least units up for auction, it is to our advantage. With some storage unit companies, we can bid $1 and win it, if we are the only one there.

Is there any way of **attending both?** We have seen another bidder, like ourselves, have a Father or Son attend auctions in their place; and if the auctioneer allows the time, they take a photo of the open storage unit, sends it and calls on the cell phone to see if they want to bid. The person bidding signs the paperwork, pays and is responsible.

I would look at **proximity** next and choose the closest if you are planning to clean out the locker and not rent it for additional time. It will save you fuel (or haul rent and fuel) and time so you can get more done in a day.

Look at the **neighborhood and safety**. Is this auction in a bad part of town and will the auction be held close to dark and do they want you to clean it out immediately? It takes some time to empty a unit, it's like moving. Is one of the sales in a safer place? Also, does the storage facility have a fence with a gate that only renters can have access to? We prefer those, but there are very few in our area.

How was your **past experience** at this location? Did you find that the items were clean (no mice, mold or dust) in the past? Did you find that clients that rent here store more expensive items? Or has there been a lot of worthless items in the past?

If you don't have as large of a **budget** to buy units, go to the sale that has the lesser amount of units; because not as many other buyers will be in attendance, and you have a better chance of getting it for a lower price.

What does the storage unit business **charge for rent** at each location? If you find that for the same size unit, let's say a 10' by 10', one is renting at $120 per month and the other is $70 per month, wouldn't you rather attend the higher rent auction? It is possible the items may be better inside.

Here is an example of how this works for **our large family**: We try and make it to both because of the great advantage of the possibility of getting a unit for $1. Try to follow me, it gets interesting!

Responsible 16-year-old child (still in driving school, so no license yet) with her cell phone and 14 year old child have been dropped off at bowling on time. Dad is at the smaller auction with a relative. Mom, 18-year-old child and baby are at the larger auction, which is a caravan auction. 20-year-old child is at home with 9, 7 and 3 year olds.

Dad's auction will be over quick, he will lock it/them up and call Mom to see where the caravan is at and join Mom at the larger auction. Mom and baby leave to join boys at bowling. Dad and the 18-year-old finish the larger auction. With our large family, we can be in four places at one time!

CHAPTER SEVEN
AUCTION DAY BEFORE THE BIDDING BEGINS

On auction morning, a few hours before the sale, call and confirm that the auction is still on and find out the address and number of the first unit to meet at. Arrive fifteen minutes early with your buddy, locks and keys, cash, light, gloves and garbage bags.

When you arrive, park somewhere you will not block access to customers' units. Walk over to where the the first unit will be auctioned and wait for the auctioneer or storage unit business owner/employee to open it.

If you have seen the show, *Storage Wars*, it looks like they cut the lock off at the sale. In our area, it does not happen that way. In fact, the storage unit owner or his/her employee cuts it off and puts their own lock on when the bill is overdue, which is weeks, months or years before the sale. For the renter to claim and reopen it, they must pay all the back rent, plus the current months' rent and possibly late fees. Plus, they may have to empty the unit immediately, as the owner of the unit business may not want to rent to them again.

If it is not a professional auctioneer, the auction is usually more relaxed and, he/she does not talk fast like an auctioneer. If it is a professional auctioneer, we have found there is often more competition because the auctioneer draws his/her own following and will advertise the sale on the auctioneer's website.

The storage unit employee/owner will open the lock with a key and pull open the door to the unit. You may look inside, but not step into it or touch anything that is right by the door. It is permissible in our area to take a photo of it on your cell phone or to shine a flashlight in it.

Sometimes, the door is opened, and the auction begins right away before you have much time to look in the unit. Other times, they give you a little or a lot more time. If there are other potential buyers, do not linger at the doorway too long. It is proper etiquette to take a quick look, then step back and let others have a look. If you are interested, and it is not too crowded, you may step up and have another look.

If there are a lot of people at the auction, many (tire kickers) are not even interested and will back off after taking a quick peek. Before the bidding starts or while the bidding is going, if you are interested in the unit, this is when everyone backs up and you have more time to look. We like to get a photo on our cell phone for this reason. We can look at the photo and enlarge certain items to be able to read a name on a box, for example, when it is crowded, and we can't look in very well over the crowd.

You can usually tell right away if the unit is clean and organized by how the boxes and totes are stacked. Have they taken care not to crush anything? Are they not stacking things too high? Do they have blankets covering a television or mirror to keep dust off and protect them?

Those are signs that someone did not want those items damaged so there is a better chance of them working and being in better shape. When you see signs of care, it provides clues that it is clean and organized and may have more valuable items.

Are there boxes that look like they have been gone through? Is there debris on the floor? Are there broken items or toys all over? Does it look like everything has been thrown inside in a hurry without a care? Are there many items that are not even in boxes that normally someone would box if they were going to store them? Is the furniture stained and ripped? Are the mattresses stained? Does it look like an unorganized mess? These are all signs that you will have a lot of garbage in this unit and there may not be many sell-able items. Don't discount the ones that are disorganized and dirty, they could still have good items in them. Make sure you are buying these at a bargain price. And consider in your mind the cost to dispose of the garbage and extra time to go through the trash in the unit and run to the dump and back many times. Is it worth it?

While you are looking at the unit considering what to bid, look for items you know you can resell and estimate in your mind what you will realistically get for them. Next, count how many boxes or bags you see and guess at their value. For example, you might think $5 per box and $2 per bag. Estimate about how many there are and do the math and add that to the amount you will get for other items. That's how much income you might get.

Also consider how many plastic totes there are with matching lids. In our area, people love to buy these for moving purposes. Within the last month, we sold 20 totes with lids (approximately 18 gallon size) on Facebook to a buyer for $80. If you know you will get $4 a piece, include that in your possible income total.

Look to see if there is something your family needs in the unit. At one time, we needed a washer. We saw in the auction listing that there was a front-load washer and dryer. This auction, at an indoor storage facility, looked very clean. The washer and dryer appeared to be in good shape, so we did pay more for that unit than we typically would have for that storage unit. We made back four times what we paid for that unit, as we sold the dryer, and many other items; and used a few other items we found in it.

Now consider expenses. Each vehicle load of garbage, depending on your disposal facility, could cost between $15 - $75 per vehicle load. There might be set prices on mattresses, televisions, microwaves, refrigerators and furniture if those items are damaged. Take the projected income minus expenses.

Consider the gas you may have to pay, rental of a trailer or moving truck, etc. Maybe you will have to rent the unit for a month until you can get everything out.

What can you earn? Now bid up to a third of that but stay in your budgeted amount. You do what you want with your money, but here's an example of why it's a third. With the money you receive as profit, after paying expenses, you may want to donate 10%, save 10%, 15% may go to pay taxes, 30% to buy your next unit, 15% to pay your household bills and expenses and 20% to pay employees/helpers, including yourself. Hopefully, you will gain more than you expect to.

CHAPTER EIGHT
TO BID AND WIN THE UNIT AND MORE

You want to win more than just the unit. You can win new friends and helpers too. Pay attention to what is going on around you. You want to win over the auctioneer/storage unit facility owner, other buyers and the units.

The *auctioneers and owners are important to win over* because they will pay attention to your bidding and be more patient with you when you are trying to make a bid if you build a reputation with them and they have good feelings towards you. Also, the owner may give you more time to get out of a unit or give you a discount on rent if you need to rent the unit for a time.

When you attend your very first auction, determine in your mind to *let the first unit or two be won by someone else* unless you are the only one there. This gives you a chance to *watch how it goes*.

Cultures (or social habits) are just a tiny bit different everywhere and your local storage auction experience may be different based on where you live.

Pay attention to conversations between the people, how they are dressed, if some appear more friendly than others. Watch your body language. Are your arms crossed? You don't want to send a signal that you are not cordial.

Get to know the other buyers like yourself. Pay attention to what they normally buy. That information can be useful and save you money. If you are not interested in a unit, but you see something in it that you know another buyer normally likes to find in units, discreetly point it out to him/her. This may cause him/her to bid higher for that unit and will take up some of that buyer's budget so he/she can't bid as high on another unit you may want that day. In return for the favor, he/she may point out items that you like.

Something you will notice as you get to know other buyers is that each person has their own "niche" of certain items they like to buy. Mostly because they have had success in getting money out of these types of items. It will be easier if your niche is not the same as your competitors, but there may be some items you both like and could get into a bidding war. Remember not to go over your budget!

Unlike the *Storage Wars* show, we find that it is better to be kind to our competition. We offer them a helping hand when they look like they need it and speak kindly to them. We even have some of their phone numbers now and they have helped us in return.

There are times that we need something, and they find it in one of their units for us. Also, some of them know how many children we have and give us children's clothing and items they find, which saves us money.

However, there are some bidders that really are competitive and will bid you up or be rude to you. Treat everyone with respect and the way you want to be treated. That person really doesn't hurt us if we stand firm and do not go over our budgeted amount.

Now, let's talk about *bidding and winning the unit*! Sometimes, no one else is interested in the unit. If you want it, place a bid for $1.00. Keep in mind the storage unit facility just wants this emptied to rent it out again, and if this is not sold, they will have to pay someone by the hour to empty it. You may get it, unless the storage unit owner has a minimum.

If you and others are interested, the auctioneer/employee will go back and forth between two to three people until the highest amount is reached, then someone else may bid even higher.

To be considerate to other potential buyers and to leave a good impression on the storage unit company for future auctions, always be polite, do not use profanity and do not to take too long in making a decision when bidding.

If you do not win the auction for that unit, yet you want something in it, make an offer for that item to the new owner. They may accept it and you will have the item you want without the hassle of cleaning out the unit.

If you do win the unit, you will be asked to pay and fill out some paperwork. Keep in mind that at some businesses you may have to pay sales tax on top of the bid price. This is usually done right at the door where you just won the bid, in our area. You may or may not receive a receipt. If you intend to do this for a business and would likely earn over $400 per year, ask for a receipt for tax purposes. You may be asked to go to the storage unit business office to get one.

Shut the door to the auctioned unit you won, lock it with your lock and don't lose the key. Write the unit number, address, and code number on your key to that lock on paper or on your cell phone memo, also write the date and time you need to be out of that unit.

Then it's on to the next unit, and the next. If it is a caravan auction, the employee may give you a list of the addresses and units to be auctioned in order. When the bidding is done at one facility, you follow the group in your own vehicle to the next facility, which may be in another town. The employee will tell you when you need to be out of the unit by. Keep track of the units you won and locked up.

CHAPTER NINE
CLEANING OUT THE UNIT

If the storage unit business owner gives you plenty of time to get out of the unit, use it to your advantage. Take photos and measurements of large items in the unit and post them on your favorite selling site like Craigslist or a Facebook selling group. You can research how to do that on each site's information page.

When people contact you, you can sell it right out of the unit. The buyer may buy other items out of the unit as well. This is less hauling for you. Sometimes they buy something we were thinking we might have to pay to dispose of.

After the auction, if you have the time, get out of the unit right away. If not, come back later with your hauling vehicle, moving buddy, flashlight, rubber gloves, tape measure and garbage bags.

Keep your rental receipt and track your mileage for tax purposes. Check with your accountant to find out all the items that are deductible in your area for this business and keep track. Schedule a time on your calendar to do this weekly or monthly and keep tax items in one "tax area" or "tax tote" so you can find it easily when "tax recording" next comes up on your calendar.

Sometimes units are a mess and you must pick up garbage off the floor and put it in the trash bags just so you can walk through it. Put on your rubber gloves and pick up all the loose items you can. Put trash in trash bags and put items to sort in other bags or half-filled containers or boxes you find in the unit.

If you have days to get out of the unit, take photos on your smartphone of the larger items you would like to sell right out of the unit. Be sure to write down measurements, brand name, model number, year manufactured, etc. to assist in looking up prices these items are selling for and to help in listing the item to sell.

With large items, we are in a Facebook rummage sale group where you can list the items you have to sell (for free) and communicate with a potential buyer through Facebook on your arrangements to meet to sell it.

We sometimes list items on Craigslist (for free) to reach potential buyers who may search Craigslist but are not a Facebook user. We list it there with the photo, measurements, details and price. Get resourceful and creative and find ways to advertise for free.

Take your buddy and the key to your lock and meet the potential client at the storage unit at the pre-determined time. Be patient with the buyer and give them time to look it over. Always remember to ask the potential buyers to look around to see if there is anything else they are interested in. We have sold many items we were intending to throw away in this fashion, which saved us on transportation and disposal costs. If the person mentions they are looking for something, keep note of that with their name and method of contacting them in case you find one someday.

If you don't have days to get out of the unit, first look around to estimate how much garbage you have. If there is about enough for a load, load it all up and take it to the dump for the first trip.

Next, try to take as much as you can in one load. If it looks like it will be more than one load, take all the smaller items to your sort facility first, then large items in the last trip.

Always be out of the unit before the deadline and clean out the unit as best you can to keep a good reputation with the storage unit owners. Because we have left a good impression on unit owners, we have been contacted and offered a unit if no one showed at an auction or if a renter wanted to give up the unit because it was owned by a deceased family member.

Sometimes we don't even have to pay when the owner gives it up and the storage unit owners are happy to have it cleared by a reliable person.

When you are out of a unit that you have been given days or weeks to get out of, contact the storage unit business owner to let them know you are out so they can rent it to another person. We have known other auction buyers who were not out on time, or that did not empty it completely that were banned from purchasing more units from the facility.

When you bring the re-sellable items to your storage area, put them all in your "incoming" section. Take photos and measurements of any large items and advertise those items right away (Craigslist, Facebook, newspaper for example). You want those to get out of your way to make it easier to get to the boxes to sort through.

Also, you might as well have people coming over to see the large items while you are there sorting the other items. Don't forget to ask if there is anything else they are looking for! That makes it less for you to have to figure out how to sell later.

CHAPTER TEN
STORAGE

If your items were loose or in bags, you will want to put them in an 18 gallon storage tote for storage until you can sort them. Take each container to your storage area.

The ideal storage area for these totes is to have four sections: "incoming", "outgoing", "re-sorting" and "big sale". You could have sections of a garage, shed or barn, a garage for each, storage sheds or tents for each (we have purchased high quality storage tents, that stayed up all year even with cold and snow 6 months of the year, for less than $200 each, see if it's okay to have them where you live) or maybe a combination of these.

"Incoming" items are those that are just coming from a storage unit you purchased and have not been sorted yet. Place totes, boxes, luggage, bags and containers toward the back and furniture and large items toward the front. You want the furniture and large items in front so that they are easier to get to if someone comes to see them from your ad. Leave yourself a path to get back to the smaller containers. Make sure that path is wide enough to carry containers out with you for sorting.

The "outgoing" section is for items that have already been sorted. They will be in labeled 18 gallon plastic storage totes (sometimes larger – use what you get from units, don't buy any, you will have more than you need soon enough!). Store these totes with the labels facing out so you can see them. Also organize them within that area.

For example, stack four "Plato's Closet" totes on top of each other. To the right of that, you may have only two "Once Upon A Child" totes stacked. To the right, you may have eight "Style Encore" totes. To the right of that, only one "Play It Again Sports" tote, and to the right of that three "Pawn Store" totes. In your space, you may need a walking path down the middle and have these totes stacked to the right and left with the labels facing the aisle.

We hate to have a "re-sorting" section. This would be our smallest area. This is for the items that are rejected (or, our "no thank yous", as one local consignment store calls them) or items that come back unsold. A person could just take these items to donate and trash and not have to store them.

We like to get money in every possible way before giving up. You have to have a place to put them because life gets busy. When you get them home, you may have to take a child to a sporting, school, or club event. Or, it may be someone's birthday, etc. When you have time to get back to this section to deal with these items, you could sort these items into separate totes in lots and mark them "Online Auction" and put them in the "outgoing" section. Or, price them for a rummage sale or huge consignment sale accordingly and move them to the "big sale" section.

The last section is the "big sale" section. Here is where you would keep items for a rummage sale, swap meet, flea market, or group consignment sale. Price your items according to the rules for each sale and label totes.

In this section, we keep books and educational items marked "Home school Sale". The local sale we take them to is only once per year. They require us to put our last name and price on the items and we sell them at our own table (which we pay a small fee to use). We recommend using blue painter's tape on books and DVDs for pricing as it removes without damaging the items.

Another type of item in our "big sale" section is "Kids Sale" items. These are large children's consignment sales that have hundreds of consignors bringing items to sell in a great big building. It may be held in a dry indoor ice hockey arena, an indoor soccer field, concert center, fairgrounds exhibitor building, etc. Some examples are Just Between Friends (JBF), Munchkin Markets, Here We Grow Again, and Green Whimsy.

The kids sale company puts up racks for clothing with sizes marked and tables with labels such as "infant toys", "toddler toys", "blocks", "cars/trucks", "breastfeeding items", "diaper bags", "shoes", etc. You, the consignor, would register to sell at the sale, pay a small fee for your portion of their advertising, price the items according to their website rules (usually with a bar code tag that you print from your printer when you are on their website), you bring your items at the drop off time indicated, they are inspected by a sale volunteer, you take the accepted items to the proper racks or tables and set them out for sale. They sell them for you all weekend.

During the sale you can see what sold on the website under your account and you come back and pick up your items at the designated pick up time. You receive a check within two weeks for 60 to 70% of the sale price. Sadly, we have to drive from one to three hours to get to one of these sales as there is not one closer to us. Usually, you can save unsold items for the next sale. There are often two sales per year at each location. Sometimes they only take spring items at the "Spring Sale" and fall items at the "Fall Sale". If you have enough locations around you, you could do a sale every weekend for about four months out of the year.

We also keep rummage sale items in the "big sale" section. After we have tried to sell in other ways, our last resort is the rummage sale. We take the time and price the items, then put them in a tote marked "Yard Sale". Then we leave it in that section until sale week. Then we take them all out and set up for the sale. It is a good idea to keep tables, doors, boards (whatever you use for tables), clothing racks, paper or plastic bags for customer purchases, signs and a chair or two in this section. We advertise our sale on many Facebook sale groups, home school websites, Craigslist, local newspaper, signs hanging in the library and restaurants. The last few hours of our sale, we offer a certain price for as many items as they can fit in the bag. That has been very successful in helping us clean up the sale!

What's left after the sale, we donate or trash. Get creative and look for other group sales to sell at. Maybe you love Matchbox cars or Legos or Trains and you could find a local sale for those items. We chose children's items to be our niche because we have eight children and we always seem to find these items in almost every unit.

CHAPTER ELEVEN
SORTING

A good place to sort is a huge table. You need to have lots of trash bags and rubber gloves ready. Have empty 18 gallon plastic totes with lids and a way to label them. Basically, you are going to bring in one box or container at a time and go through it and sort it's contents to one of three places: trash, donate, or one of your totes (if small enough to fit) to resell.

We have two places for trash. We put smaller trash in plastic 13 gallon bags and empty cardboard boxes on the porch to keep them dry until our local dump is open (two days a week). We put the larger trash items next to the garage to make it easier to load into the vehicle.

It always amazes us how much trash we find. Even a clean, organized and neatly packed (by a moving company) unit will have items that have been broken during the move or items with stains, rips, holes, paperwork, etc. There are many personal items that do not sell such as old school papers, expired coupons, old mail, newspapers, magazines, etc. Always get a receipt if you pay for trash disposal for tax purposes.

Keep your morals rather than the money. We put things we would not feel right about buying or do not promote in the trash. Some may say it is good money down the drain, but if it causes someone else to fall into sin, temptation or harm themselves or someone else (like a recalled toy or high chair), it is not worth any amount of money, so we have more trash.

The items that are to be donated, we put in cardboard boxes (from units, don't buy them, you will soon have too many) labeled with donation centers like Salvation Army, Goodwill, Habitat for Humanity ReStore etc. and load those in the vehicle to drop off right away. If we have a lot of them and the donation center is not open, they spend the night on the porch.

When you find the good items that will be resold, check their condition and clean them if necessary. You may need to put new batteries in electronic items. You may need to plug in electronic items to be sure they are in working order. You will label the totes as you put items into them.

Storage Business Where You Bought The Unit – If you find birth certificates, high school or college degrees, baby books, and photographs, you put them in here and take it back to the owner of the storage unit business and ask them to keep you anonymous and they will contact the old owner to come and get these items by a certain time or they will toss them. It is up to you if you want to do this or not.

Hangers – Save these for group consignment sales, both child size and adult size.

Categories – All other items will be sorted into categories to sell online or take to certain places to get money for them. See the next chapter for more information.

CHAPTER TWELVE
WHERE TO SELL THE GOOD STUFF

Below are some business names or types to label your totes and what goes in them. (Businesses may be named something else in your area, label accordingly.)

The Gold Guy – (local gold, silver and jewelry buyer – pays cash on the spot) jewelry, watches, etc.

Play It Again Sports – (sports resale store – pays cash on the spot) slightly to gently used, modern sports and exercise balls and equipment such as weights for weight lifting or aerobics items, sports shoes, helmets, pads, rackets, baseball or softball bats and other related items, hockey items, football items, volleyball nets, balls, tennis, golf items, etc.

Pawn Store – (will give you credit or cash on the spot) knives, jewelry (last place we take jewelry before our rummage sale), small appliances, musical instruments, speakers, CD or DVD players, electronics, cell phones, cameras, DVDs (save empty cases for best resale value in case you find DVDs to go in them someday, most will only take them if they are in a case), etc.

Gaming Stores – (will give you credit or cash on the spot) these stores love vintage or modern video games (save empty cases in case you find game to go in them someday for best resale value), video game systems, iPods, iPads, tablets, etc.

Cards & Comics Shop – (credit or cash) trading cards such as sports or specialty cards (like baseball cards or Pokemon cards), comic books, collector memorabilia, etc.

Music Resale Shop – (credit or cash onsite) music CDs, records, albums if in good shape, etc.

The Book Resale Shop – (you get credit or cash onsite, not very common) books and audio books (we try to sell the ones we think will go well on eBay or take kids, educational and teen books to home school or group consignment sales first)

Local or Regional Online Auction – (this is an online auction house that sells items for you online, you pay a small fee and they get a percent of sales) knick knacks, craft supplies, fishing equipment, remaining sports collectibles, items not chosen at other places put into a "lot", empty storage containers, sewing machines, small appliances, chairs, plant stands, just about anything someone else might want to buy, etc.

Once Upon A Child – (or your local consignment store, cash on the spot) This is a store that buys gently used kids stuff. You bring in your items (no appointment necessary), they review your items, choose items they want, they offer you payment for all items accepted. Some items they take are clothing (newborn to Kids 16), outerwear, costumes, dance wear, sleepwear, toys, books, outdoor toys, ride on toys, puzzles, games, shoes, boots, dance shoes, rain boots, snow boots, special occasion shoes, strollers, high chairs, play yards, entertainers, swings maternity, nursing bras, nursing shawls, front and back infant carriers, etc. They do not buy car seats, formula, recalled items, or stuffed animals.

Plato's Closet – (or your local consignment store, cash on the spot) This store buys gently used brand name current clothing and accessories for teens and young adults. They take girls clothing size 0 to 16, Guys clothing size 28 – 40 waist, jeans, shirts, tops, pants, shorts, t-shirts, tanks, sweaters, hoodies, dresses, shoes, boots, sandals, sneakers, jewelry (we take jewelry to a gold buyer first, then here second), belts, scarves, purses, backpacks, book bags, sunglasses, gloves, coats, jackets and hats.

Style Encore – (or your local consignment store, cash on the spot) They buy gently used clothing and accessories for fashion conscious, spending savvy women. No appointment is necessary, and they pay on the spot. They buy women's clothing 0 – 3X, jeans, shirts, tops, pants, shorts, blazers, dresses, shoes, boots, sandals, coats, jackets, belts, scarves, handbags, skirts, active wear, purses and jewelry (we take jewelry here third).

Local Home Consignment Store – Some of these decide which items they will try to sell in their store, and you get paid when it sells. They may have a website, where you can look online anytime to see if you have money to pick up. They contact you when unwanted items are ready to be picked up. If you are particular on price, you may include a list. (We let them price for us.) You receive percentage of the sale. At our local store, for furniture, they request a photo prior to bringing the item in to see if they want it there or not. Our location accepts excellent condition and trendy home décor, furniture, lamps, rugs, kitchen tools, current serving-ware, like new linens, architectural salvage, shabby chic, garden art, choice antiques, children's décor, select purses, handbags, and accessories (we don't take jewelry here), art, etc.

eBay/Amazon – Items we intend to sell on this site. It may include sports jerseys, autographed items, collectibles, books, movies, video games, DVDs, Blu-rays, basically items we think we can get more money from selling here than at the other places. Sometimes we try to sell an item here and end up taking it somewhere else when it doesn't sell.

Etsy – handmade crafts (that you make out of materials found in the unit, if you are crafty) craft supplies and vintage items over 20 years old.

Money – keep a ziploc bag of money, gift cards, gift certificates, foreign coins/bills. Look through those papers and birthday cards! We have found money and gift certificates or gift cards in them. Amy really enjoyed the manicure and bottles of fingernail polish she got from a gift certificate in a unit. Mike really enjoyed his savings at Famous Dave's restaurant from a gift card too. This is what makes this business fun!

Keys – save every key you find in a ziploc bag until you are through the entire unit. You may find a fireproof safe, a lock box, a locked jewelry box, locked gun case, trigger lock on a gun, etc. that you will need the key for. When you are through the unit, if the keys are not used, decide if you want to wait to see if another unit with this previous owner's name will show up or toss them.

Mystery Remote controls & cords – save any of these that you find until you are through the unit, then move them to pawn or eBay. You may find an item a remote goes to as you go through the unit. We save some of these a long time, which pays off if we find a great TV without a cord, then we look in our cords box and have one!

CHAPTER THIRTEEN
SELLING

You have purchased the items and sorted through them and have taken the donation and trash items to where they go. Now it is time to see what money you can get out of the good stuff. Hopefully, people have already been coming to buy your large items and maybe you have already made your money back on the unit just from selling the large items.

Now sit down and think. Write down the business names of places you need to take totes to and how many totes for each business.

We recommend only bringing two boxes a day to pawn, resale or consignment stores so as to not overwhelm them. Also, they seem to take more items that way than when you bring in more boxes. Please keep in mind that it sometimes depends on the worker looking at the items. With bringing less boxes on different days, you will get a variety of workers. One worker may only buy one item from you out of two boxes. You bring the same two boxes another day and you will only have a half box left to take home.

This business can still work out even if you have a day job. Plan out your week. Maybe you can drop some off each day on a lunch hour or after work. Or, if you have a few days open and a large vehicle, you can drop off several in one day.

Sometimes, the store employees will go through it while you are there. Other times, you may have to come back in a few hours or at the end of the day depending on the business.

At some consignment places or online auction businesses, you will drop it off and leave it for days or months until sold or returned.

A gold/silver buyer may need you to make an appointment so you will have to plan when you can do that as well. As you take items to pawn and consignment stores more often, you will come to understand what they will or won't buy from you or sell for you.

When items come back, price them for either a large group consignment sale according to that company's rules, for a rummage sale, or donate or trash them.

In the evenings and weekends, you can meet people to sell large items or items you have on a local Facebook sale page or Craigslist. You can also list items on sites like eBay, Amazon or Etsy. You will need to research these sites on your own to see their current listing and selling fees and how to do them.

CHAPTER FOURTEEN
TAXES

Get a receipt book and a mileage tracking book from an office supply store. When someone purchases an item from you in person, write a receipt and keep a copy.

If you are on a site like eBay, you can print a copy of the invoice or print out a report in the finances section.

If you sell at a group consignment sale, you will get a check stub so keep track of those. Pawn stores and resale stores will give you a receipt for what they pay you for your items. Keep track of all income.

Keep track of all of your receipts for supplies, the storage unit auction purchase price paid (sometimes you have to go to their office to get this), garbage disposal, mileage, equipment (example: measuring tape, flashlight, storage tent, etc.) and whatever else your accountant thinks you should keep track of.

We keep all our new, incoming receipts in an empty ice cream container. You will frequently need to go through the receipts and list them under departments like income, supplies, garbage, equipment, etc.

We recommend hiring an accountant for the business and keep all the receipts for what you pay that person as a business expense too. They have the time to keep up on all the laws and know how often you will need to report your earnings. It may be once a year or 4 times a year. It might depend on what you are earning.

CHAPTER FIFTEEN
PRIVACY

In this business, we have had times where we didn't want to tell anyone what we were doing for several reasons. What if the person you are talking to knows someone who lost their storage unit and we bought it? Or what if they themselves have defaulted on a storage locker in the past? That would be awkward.

What if they want to do this too and decide to start coming to the auctions? Then we will have more competition and have to pay higher prices. What if they judge us or our children thinking that everything we wear is used? We do buy some new clothing (especially socks, underwear and swimsuits) and shoes and have the receipts to prove it, but we *love* the savings when we can find items in units.

Now that we have been doing this for a while, it is part of our life and we treat it like a family business and are more open to talking about it. If we ever do discover that the person we are talking to or their buddy has lost one, we would try and comfort them. It would be very hard to go through for sure. But, you will have to decide for yourself whether you want to tell others about it or not. When we weren't telling people, and they asked where we got something, we simply said, "at an auction".

Some of the pros with telling people is that you can ask them if they are looking for anything or need anything and you can decide if you want to write down what they are looking for and call them when you find it. Or, if you want to bless someone.

We had an old friend who went through a house fire and we were able to offer many items for free as we had already gotten our money back on the unit by selling some large items. If your kids have friends going off to college, you can help them if you find a microwave, loft bed, desk, lamp, etc. You could charge them the price of helping you clean out a unit. If your church youth group is having a rummage sale to earn money for a missions trip, you will have many items to donate.

CHAPTER SIXTEEN
SUMMARY & RESOURCES

Summary

We never stop learning in this business. There are always new items we find that we have to figure out, how do I get money out of this? We learn new tips and tricks from other storage auction buyers. You may have noticed by now that they don't want to give you any information because you are a competitor to them. After you are kind to them for a few years, that may change and you may share secrets and help one another.

You learned all about preparing yourself ahead of the time for the sale, how to budget, what to bring with you to an auction, how an auction works, cleaning out the unit, selling the items, storage, sorting, how to make money selling the items, paying taxes and privacy.

You have all the tips you need to get out there and work this business. Today could be the day that you attend an auction, make a purchase and find a treasure. This week you could sell all the profitable items and can be making money buying storage units! We hope you enjoyed this book and are more prepared than we were in starting this new journey.

Resources

Please go to our website to see what we recommend that you purchase to help you in your business as well as other resources.

https://neededinthehome.com/storage-units-resources

Happy treasure hunting!

ABOUT THE AUTHORS

Mike and Amy Marohl met in college in 1994, where they both received Associates Degrees in Marketing. They married in 1996 and have eight children. Mike is a sports card collector and re-seller. Amy enjoys crafting and selling her creations at local craft shows and has authored other books/journals that can be found on Amazon.